EAST ANGLIA
IN COLOUR

JOHN WORRALL

DIAL
HOUSE

First published 1996

ISBN 0 7110 2454 5

© John Worrall 1996

Published by Dial House

an imprint of Ian Allan Ltd, Terminal House, Station Approach, Shepperton, Surrey TW17 8AS; and printed by Ian Allan Printing Ltd, Coombelands House, Coombelands Lane, Addlestone, Surrey KT15 1HY.

Front cover:
Blakeney, North Norfolk
The port of Blakeney on the North Norfolk coast carried substantial commercial trade in the Middle Ages but silting of the Channel eventually put paid to most of it. Now, a pretty village of narrow streets and flint buildings, it receives an increasing number of leisure sailors, birdwatchers and holiday makers.

Back cover:
Horsey Mill, Northeast Norfolk
Horsey Mill at Horsey Staithe on the eastern fringe of the Norfolk Broads is owned by the National Trust and is open to the public during daylight hours through the summer. Formerly part of the Broads drainage system, it is a windpump, a device for lifting water to a higher level, rather than a windmill which grinds grain.

Title page:
Cromer Pier, Norfolk

Right:
Debenham, Suffolk
Debenham, at the head of the River Deben and a former wool town, is in a part of Suffolk which, at the time of the Norman invasion was, together with central Norfolk, one of the two most densely populated parts of England. Its main street contains a number of fine timber-framed buildings.

INTRODUCTION

Geology, geography and history have dealt East Anglia a useful hand.

It is a place of big skies, rich soils, slow rivers and small estuarine ports, a quiet place, close enough to London and the Midlands to be accessible but mostly too far to be anyone's dormitory.

When glaciation last remodelled the region's geological face a mere 10–20,000 years ago, it left a landscape of soft alluvial sediments with a sense of space but little vertical dimension. The land hardly rises above 400ft and most is much lower.

Much of it is also very fertile except for remarkable Breckland which, in its natural state, was sandy heathland, a relative desert complete with the occasional sandstorm. Now improved, it is largely arable, with some land put down to conifer forests around Thetford, or used by the Ministry of Defence and closed to the public since the 1920s.

Prodigiously fertile by contrast are the Fens, the flatlands running south from the coast of the Wash comprising much of Cambridgeshire and West Norfolk. Once a massive glacial lake turned swamp and now with a soil bed shrunk by centuries of drainage, they are mostly below mean high-water mark. The canals and drains which draw off the water are encased in embankments above the surrounding black-soiled fields. Fortunately perhaps, East Anglia's climate is the driest in the country.

The sea still threatens, nevertheless. Since the ice withdrew, the soft sedimentary rocks — if they can be called rocks — have been shaped to form coast by the flooding of the North Sea basin. The process continues. Erosion is a problem from the Wash to the Orwell, and beyond.

But the sea has brought prosperity, and invaders, too — often hand in hand. The Romans were here and their roads and remains litter the place. They moved north, completing their routes to the coast probably after the little local difficulty with Boadicea. The Saxons who followed were more settlers than colonists, forming the Anglo-Saxon race and the kingdom of East Anglia itself with its North Folk (Norfolk) and South Folk (Suffolk). But like the Danes who followed them, they built mostly in wood and left little for modern day archaeologists. One spectacular exception was the Sutton Hoo burial site near Woodbridge in Suffolk.

The Normans in contrast used stone and did better on the legacy stakes. Many of their churches and cathedrals are still in use, as are some of their castles if only in recreational and educational contexts.

Economically, East Anglia has played on its strengths. It cornered the medieval wool industry with good pasture and proximity to European markets notably the Netherlands; the Dutch reciprocated with craftsmen. In that period, East Anglia was the most prosperous and populous part of England with particular concentrations in Suffolk. As a result, today, many small towns have fine ancient buildings to show.

With the onset of mechanisation, wool moved to the Pennines where faster streams could power the machinery. East Anglia then turned to agriculture and has stayed with it. There was no coal or iron with which to join the Industrial Revolution and so the region developed no major conurbations; its biggest centre, Norwich, has a population of 128,000.

Indeed, East Anglia is now the least populous region of England but it does have the best farmland and an even spread of villages and towns. In Norfolk, in winter, when the leaves have gone, half a dozen church towers might be visible from one slightly elevated point.

Little seems likely to change, despite the quickening pace of national life. East Anglia is essentially a cul-de-sac with a road system indifferent to worldly haste. The M11 heading first north-eastwards from London, only brushes the region, veering northwest past Cambridge to join the A14, having long ago achieved its objective of making the Government's pre-ordained Stansted airport decision more plausible.

The A14, for its part, is a major European route, connecting the Midlands to Felixstowe, Britain's biggest container port, but its massive and increasing traffic stays on that hardened artery bringing only peripheral noise and fumes and not much disturbing of the peace.

The rest of East Anglia works with a mix of single and dual carriageways, sometimes congested in the caravan season but otherwise not unduly burdened. Norwich has no complete dual carriageway connection with the rest of the country and seems unlikely to get one, a fact sporadically decried by some sections of commerce, but appreciated as a tempering influence by others.

For after agriculture come visitors, and East Anglia caters for a

Previous page:
Ramsey Abbey, Cambridgeshire
This monastic gatehouse fragment, built about 1500 and now preserved by the National Trust, is all that remains of Ramsey Abbey. It is open to the public. Behind it, Ramsey Grammar School has incorporated the Abbey's 13th century Lady Chapel which is not open to the public.

Above:
Snape Maltings, Snape, Suffolk
Snape Maltings sit at the tidal limit of the River Alde near the Suffolk coast. The old malting house was converted to a concert hall in 1967 and became the centrepiece of the Aldeburgh Festival. It was gutted by fire on the first night of the 1969 festival but was rebuilt in time for the opening of the 1970 season.

Right:
Towards Cawston, Northeast Norfolk
An area of originally dense woodland, the land in central Northeast Norfolk was converted piecemeal to arable use and gradually enclosed. By the end of the 16th century, only 10% of the parish of Cawston was farmed in open fields. One result is that straight stretches of road such as this are the exception, the otherwise mostly tortuous system of country lanes having evolved slowly around the small fields which predominated in the area.

category that tends to produce repeat business. What it has to offer it wants to keep exclusive. There may even be some reassurance for those making a necessarily steady pace eastwards along the A17 and A47, or north-eastwards on the single carriageway sections of the A11, that nothing worthwhile comes easy and that the hordes may thus be deterred a little.

There is only one brash coastal resort in East Anglia, but Yarmouth serves its market well and still offers a wealth of history to those who would look for just a while beyond the beach and the slot-machines. It is also a major port for the offshore oil industry. The Broads can have their hectic weeks, but they are there the year round for visitors preferring a quieter pace.

Southwold, Hunstanton and Cromer are each from different moulds while small North Norfolk ports such as Blakeney, Wells and Brancaster have more or less retired from commercial maritime endeavour and now set their creek moorings, flint cottages and pubs at the disposal of weekend sailors who often use them more than they do the sea itself. But that's fair enough; the sea is the sea but some of these places are special.

Throw in the Fens, the architecture and the history and add some first-class birdwatching, and East Anglia has a diversity which most residents can barely expect to sample completely, let alone any visitor with a time limitation. Hopefully this book will show something of what has had to be foregone so far.

THE EAST ANGLIAN COAST

Left:
The Norfolk coast at Terrington Marsh on the southern fringe of the Wash, close to the Lincolnshire border; a bleak place of scattered farms, earth banks and saltmarsh. This is part of 'Marshland', the product of periodical sea inundation, as opposed to 'Fenland' further south which was subjected to seasonal flooding by fresh water.

Above:
The Custom House, King's Lynn
The Custom House is one of 'Lynn's' most noted buildings. Built by Henry Bell, an architect and mayor of Lynn in 1683, for Sir John Turner, a local vintner; it sits beside a small dock off the River Great Ouse.

Left:

Waterfront, King's Lynn, Norfolk.

Fishing boats tied up on the River Great Ouse, King's Lynn, are part of an industry in difficulty. Nearly 100 boats are based at the port working the Wash for cockles, mussels and shrimp but while larger boats such as these kept working, many smaller boats are laid up at any one time. Mussel stocks have fallen; cockle quotas provide work for only part of the year and shrimp migrations have become erratic. It is not yet clear whether shrimp behaviour is due to warmer summers or off-shore dredging for sand to bolster eroding beaches.

Above:

Hunstanton, Norfolk

The Victorian resort of Hunstanton grew with the coming of the railway in 1862 It was developed just to the south of the original village — now known as Old Hunstanton — by local land owners, the L'Estrange family, and many of its buildings are of local carstone, a distinctive brown sandstone. Today it is a small but very popular family resort on East Anglia's only west-facing coast.

Left:
Burnham Overy Staithe, North Norfolk
Overy Staithe is one of the small North Norfolk ports which once had a commercial significance but silting and tidal restrictions long ago turned it almost entirely to leisure sailing.

Above:
Wells-next-the-Sea, North Norfolk
During the reign of Elizabeth I, Wells was the leading port in North Norfolk but again silting of the Channel became increasingly restricting. Small fishing boats still operate but activity is otherwise centred mainly on the leisure sector. The bank from the town quay to the point, seen here, was built by the Earl of Leicester of nearby Holkham Hall in 1859. He also planted the pines which now consolidate the dunes of Holkham Meals immediately to the west.

Right:
Wells Beach
Two backpackers make their way past the beach huts towards the pines and dunes of Holkham Meals in the evening.

Far right:
Blakeney Point, North Norfolk
The seals prepare to receive more visitors. Blakeney Point, a sandspit and nature reserve, is accessible by a lengthy walk from Blakeney quay, but the foreshore area frequented by the seals is off-limits. Boat trips for seal spotters run from the quay and from nearby Morston Quay.

Far left:
Cley-next-the-Sea, North Norfolk
Cley was another thriving port until
local landowners interfered with the
flow of the River Glaven in the
17th century in an attempt to convert
estuarine saltings to grazing. A
petition to the Privy Council saw
the bank removed but trade never
recovered and when a bank was
built across the estuary in the early
19th century, the harbour quickly
silted up. Only small leisure craft use
Cley now.

Left:
Sheringham, North Norfolk
Like Hunstanton, Sheringham
developed on the strength of the
railway connection, but unlike
Hunstanton, it still has trains.
Regular services connect with
Norwich while the North Norfolk
Railway operates steam and diesel
services on a 5-mile stretch of line
between Sheringham and the
outskirts of Holt.

15

Far left:
**Mammuthus trogontherii,
West Runton, North Norfolk**
In 1990, the remains of a
600,000 year-old early species
of mammoth the size of a
double-decker bus were found
at the foot of the cliffs at West
Runton between Sheringham
and Cromer. Some bones were
recovered in 1992 and the
excavation was completed
during the autumn of 1995. A
find of international
importance, some remains are
on exhibition at the Castle
Museum, Norwich. The rest
will be displayed when
analysis has been completed.

Left:
Cromer Pier, Norfolk
Cromer, another family resort
in the Victorian railway
mould, is big enough to offer
traditional end-of-pier
entertainment although it is
also known for its crab-fishing
industry. The town's church
has the highest tower, 160ft,
(48.75m) in Norfolk.

17

Above:

Great Yarmouth, East Norfolk

Yarmouth is the major family holiday resort of East Anglia but it had already had a long career before the entertainment piers and boarding houses arrived. Built substantially on a spit of land between the River Yare and the sea, Yarmouth had a town wall with 18 towers completed by 1400. Parts of the wall and several towers remain. The town was once a major herring port but is now heavily involved in servicing the off-shore oil and gas industries.

Right:

The Trawl Dock, Lowestoft, Suffolk

Lowestoft remains synonymous with fishing despite the general decline of the industry; until recently, it remained the busiest fishing port in England. In terms of fish landed, it has now been overtaken by Brixham and Newlyn from which significantly more smaller longshore craft operate, but nearly 50 longshore boats and a dozen or so 'beamers' — deep sea trawlers — are still based at Lowestoft.

Right:
Southwold, Suffolk
Beach huts give this Suffolk resort an Edwardian air, but it was a fishing village in medieval times and began to grow only in the 15th century when the busier Dunwich, three miles down the coast, was being diminished by sea incursion and the blocking of its harbour. Southwold once had a railway which closed before the War and a pier which was dismantled after a battering by gales in 1978. It is now a small and genteel resort and home to the Adnams brewery.

Far right:
Walberswick, Suffolk
Early morning light falls on the jetties of the River Blyth. Across the Blyth from Southwold, Walberswick was also once a flourishing port but activity is now mainly restricted to leisure and fishing craft, and the national crab-catching championship which it hosts every summer.

Left:

Shingle Street, Suffolk

The hamlet of Shingle Street, a string of dwellings on a dead-end lane, is built on the edge of a shingle beach thrown up where the River Alde runs into the sea. In turn, bleak and peaceful, it imparts a sense of impermanence in winter storms when the shingle offshore moves constantly. Residents take comfort perhaps from the fact that two Martello towers have been there since Napoleon's time.

Above:

Woodbridge, Suffolk

Woodbridge, like nearby Ipswich, was a busy estuarine port in Elizabethan times, but the Deben was a less navigable river than the Orwell and Woodbridge failed to compete. The result is a small and pretty town with fine buildings and considerable patronage by leisure sailors. The weatherboard red-roofed tide-mill in the central background is arguably the most photographed building in Suffolk.

Right:
The Wet Dock, Ipswich
The Wet Dock was built in 1842 and was prominent in the shipment of malt to London. Ipswich, as one of the Haven ports, remains an important national cargo gateway. The county town was also the birthplace of Thomas Wolsey who was Henry VIII's Lord Chancellor and is regarded as the most powerful person to have emerged from Suffolk.

Far right:
Felixstowe, Suffolk
The resort of Felixstowe was in its prime at the end of the last century having become fashionable after a visit by the German Empress, Augusta and her children in 1891. It retains an old-fashioned charm.

THE COAST UNDER THREAT

Erosion has long been a problem on the coast of East Anglia and a number of villages and towns have disappeared during the last millennium. Many parts of the Norfolk coast remain under threat and Easton Bavents just north of Southwold in Suffolk has one of the fastest erosion rates in the country. The heart of the problem is that the coast is very young in geological terms. Soft deposits laid down during the last Ice Age have been formed into the present coastline by wave action over the last 10,000 years and the process will continue whatever man tries to do. Any defence works — sea walls for example — starve other parts of the coast of beach replenishment material, causing beach levels to drop and exposing unprotected cliffs to more direct wave action.

   Protection of every mile of coast is neither financially feasible nor ecologically desirable ; artificial defences last only a few decades at most in any case. But, just as many parts of the East coast were inundated in the disastrous floods of 1953 and 1938, and on many other occasions over the centuries, it is now generally accepted that with global warming, rising sea levels and changing wave patterns, it is only a matter of time before defences fail substantially again

Right:
Brancaster, North Norfolk
Only 30 years ago, the club house of the Royal West Norfolk Golf Club at Brancaster where the Duke of Edinburgh is patron and Prince Andrew sometimes plays, was protected by sand dunes. Now the sea has advanced to the point where the club house must shelter, for now, behind its own protective barrier of granite boulders.

Right:
Salthouse, North Norfolk
The shingle bank near Salthouse keeps the sea from the marshes and the village. But to do so, it must be maintained in winter at an artificially steep angle by mechanical diggers, and then storms steadily reduce it to equilibrium, sometimes overtopping it and inundating the freshwater marshes in the process.

Far right:
Salthouse: the freshwater marshes after overtopping.

Right:
Near Weybourne, North Norfolk
The soft and friable nature of the low coastal cliffs is illustrated here where storms make steady inroads each winter.

Far right:
Sea Palling, Northeast Norfolk
Fragile marram dunes and an ageing sea wall have until recently been the only protection for the village of Sea Palling which suffered major flooding and seven deaths during the floods of 1953. Marram is a natural defence which in theory is self-sustaining: sand blows off the beach and marram grass takes root in it, trapping more sand and growing higher. Marram dunes can rise to 60ft (20m) or more. But artificial defences can interrupt the process — a sea wall starves the dunes of more sand. Sea Palling is now seeing a major, but largely experimental, scheme to build off-shore reefs as further protection. The knock-on effect along the coast remains to be seen.

Left:
Cart Gap, Norfolk
Low sand cliffs at Cart Gap near Happisburgh (pronounced Hazebro') take a battering from winter seas. This stretch is of particular concern, having seen a 25yd (22m) incursion into the cliff during a storm in 1992. Another 75yd (70m) will take a high tide into land below mean high water mark and then into the Norfolk Broads.

Above:
Hemsby, Norfolk
A holiday bungalow at Hemsby, north of Great Yarmouth, awaits its inevitable fate. Nearly 50 such bungalows, most of them dating from the interwar period, have been lost in recent years.

Right:
Hemsby
Another bungalow at Hemsby
finally yields.

CITIES, TOWNS AND VILLAGES

Above:

Parker's Piece, Cambridge

Parker's Piece is an area of open land southeast of the city centre which was acquired by the city from Trinity College in 1613 in exchange for land west of the River Cam in the area now known as The Backs. It gets its name from Edward Parker, a cook, to whom it had been leased by the college in 1587. It is now a public open space.

Above:
Market Hill, Cambridge
The market area was originally L-shaped, according to a plan dated 1592, but a fire in 1849 destroyed buildings and prompted the corporation to clear the site. The market place took its present shape in 1855 and operates six days a week.

Right:
Punting on the River Cam, Cambridge
The River Cam, next to Magdalen Bridge, sees many a chaotic scene as visitors to the city first get to grips with the punting science.

Above:

Gonville and Caius College, Cambridge

Just off King Parade in the busiest part of the city, the courtyard of Gonville and Caius College offers contrasting peace and serenity. The college was first founded in 1348 as Gonville Hall but when Henry VIII commandeered Physwick Hostel, which was part of its student accommodation, for his new foundation, Trinity College, a former Gonville student John Caius — a Norwich man and eventually physician to three monarchs — stepped in to become master and buy more land to complete the present site. Sir Stephen Hawking wrote his best seller, *A Brief History of Time*, at the college.

Right:

Winter on the Cam

Clare Bridge dates from the 17th century and the rebuilding of Clare College. The old joke is to ask visitors to count the number of stone balls on the parapets. The answer is 13 and $^4/_5$ because one has a piece missing, the result of a bet on the same question where the potential loser cut out a segment in the middle of the night in an attempt to win on a technicality.

Right:
King's College, Cambridge
The queue for the Christmas Eve carol service in King's College Chapel — 'A Festival of Nine Lessons and Carols' — usually begins to form a couple of days before the event. College staff sometimes serve refreshments. (Photographed with kind permission of the Provost and Scholars of King's College.)

Far right:
North Brink, Wisbech, Cambridgeshire
Wisbech, in the centre of the bulb-growing area of the Cambridgeshire Fens, contains some of the county's most notable architecture outside Cambridge. North Brink, beside the River Nene, includes the houses of merchants and bankers who prospered in the town's peak of importance as a port in the 18th and 19th centuries.

Above:
Market Hill, Framlingham, Suffolk
Framlingham is a small town with a Saturday market and a deep involvement in the medieval history of England as a seat of the powerful Earls — and later — the Dukes of Norfolk. Roger Bigod, the second Earl, was one of the 25 barons who forced King John to sign the Magna Carta.

Right:
Kersey, Suffolk
Kersey is one of Suffolk's best known chocolate-box villages, a place of many thatched and timber-framed houses nestling in a dip through which a stream runs across the main street. Like many other architecturally well-endowed villages in the county, it did well from the medieval wool trade.

Far left:

Cavendish, Suffolk

Cavendish, in the Stour valley on the Essex border, has a large green which is topped by an early 14th century church tower. The village was home to Sir John Cavendish, the Chief Justice whose son stabbed Wat Tyler at Smithfield in 1381. A vengeful peasant mob went after Sir John who hid his valuables in the church tower and fled but was caught near Lakenheath and killed.

Left:

Lady Street, Lavenham, Suffolk

Lavenham is the best known of the Suffolk wool towns and, at the time of Henry VIII, was the 14th wealthiest town in England. Almost every building is an exhibit. But if today it is more looked at than lived in, and preservation for presentation seems to be the way of life, Lavenham is still regarded as one of the finest collections of late medieval architecture in the country.

Right:
Cornhill, Ipswich, Suffolk
The present day Cornhill is
the focus of the town centre of
the county town and, as
Market Place, was the central
point of the original
settlement in the 7th century.

Left:

Market Place, Norwich
There has been a market on this
site for more than 900 years.
Market tolls were first collected
at the original toll house which
stood on the site of the
Guildhall, seen here in the
background, centre right. To the
left is City Hall. Until the
introduction of shops in the 17th
century, all retailing was done
here and in subsidiary markets
in the side streets. The modern
day provision market operates
six days a week

49

Left:

Bishop Bridge, Norwich

Until recently, this bridge over the River Wensum was thought to be the oldest in England still open to traffic but vehicular traffic no longer uses it. The bridge dates from 1340 and originally carried one of the oldest routes into the city. It was the only river crossing outside the city walls and was fortified to form part of the city's defences. It was the scene of bitter fighting during the peasant uprising known as Kett's Rebellion.

Above:

Elm Hill, Norwich

Once the home of the rich and powerful of Tudor Norwich — who liked to live close to the river that brought much of the merchandise to the city — Elm Hill provided a total of 16 Norwich mayors and sheriffs from its residents. But by the beginning of this century it was a slum and would have been redeveloped in the 1930s but for the efforts of the Norwich Society. Now, with its retained cobbles and many fine restored buildings, it is perhaps the part of the city best known to visitors. The name comes from an elm tree which once stood there, but the fourth elm to carry the connection finally fell to Dutch elm disease and was replaced in 1980 by this London plane tree.

51

Above:
Worstead Festival, Norfolk
The village of Worstead gave its name, slightly altered, to the wool weave known as Worsted which was developed here when the wool industry was at its height in the Middle Ages. The fine church in what is now a small village testifies to the prosperity of those times. The village holds an annual three-day festival in high summer which attracts many visitors.

Right:
Wroxham, Norfolk
Wroxham is perhaps the principal centre of the Norfolk Broads. A boat building and hiring centre since late Victorian times, it is very busy during high season when boats putter continuously under the narrow bridge while road traffic crawls over it. But at quieter times, its waterfront terraces are very restful.

Right:
Thetford, Norfolk
Thetford's most famous son, Thomas Paine, is regarded as the most significant political writer of the late 18th century, producing a series of books and pamphlets urging political and social change and championing the rights of the common man. Born in 1737, the son of a corset maker, he moved to London at the age of 20 and then to America in 1774 where he became convinced of the need for American independence. He was involved in the American, and later the French, Revolution but his perhaps most famous publication, *The Rights of Man*, advocated, among other things, the abolition of the English monarchy and saw him outlawed at home. His statue stands in King Street.

BUILDINGS

Above:
Felbrigg Hall, Norfolk
The south wing of Felbrigg, bearing the words 'Gloria deo in excelsis', was built about 1620 for the Windham family. A number of additions and alterations were made, up to 1830. The church containing a number of brasses to members of the Felbrigg and Windham families, stands in the park a short distance to the southeast of the house. Felbrigg is owned by the National Trust and is open to the public.

Above:
Blickling Hall, Norfolk
Blickling, of similar vintage to Felbrigg, is larger and more spectacular. It was built by Sir Henry Hobart, Lord Chief Justice, within a medieval moat which was the site of the home of the Boleyn family and perhaps of Anne Boleyn, Henry VIII's second wife who was beheaded on 19 May 1536. Sir Henry was slain in a duel on Cawston Heath in 1698. Blickling is also a National Trust house

Left:
Wymondham Abbey church, Norfolk
The two towers of the abbey church of SS Mary and Thomas are the result of a 14th and 15th century dispute between the townspeople and the Abbey monks over the shared use of the church. The monks had built for themselves the octagonal tower in the foreground and put up a wall in the nave to seal themselves and the high altar from the townspeople. In 1445, work was begun on the bigger square tower to house the people's bells. But in 1538 the adjacent abbey was dissolved. The agent for its demolition, John Flowerdew, subsequently had a personal feud with the brothers William and Robert Kett which, in July 1549, sparked off the peasants' revolt against enclosures, known as Kett's Rebellion.

57

Above:

Castle Acre Priory, Norfolk

Castle Acre stands on the Peddars Way, a Roman road which runs to the North Norfolk coast. Just to the southwest of the village centre lie the remains of the Priory which was founded in 1090 by William de Warrenne, the son-in-law of William the Conqueror. It is now administered by English Heritage and is open to the public.

Above:

Wickmere church, North Norfolk

Round church towers are mostly an East Anglian phenomenon. There are 119 in Norfolk, 41 in Suffolk, eight in Essex and only 12 in the rest of the country.

They are a mixture of Saxon and Norman origins, with the majority of Norfolk's round towers, for example, thought to date from between 1015 and 1115.

Holy Trinity Church, Long Melford, Suffolk
Long Melford is regarded by many as having the most impressive single thoroughfare in Suffolk — long and wide with many fine houses. At the northern end above a wide green sits Holy Trinity church, in its turn regarded as one of the grandest Perpendicular churches in Suffolk. The adoption of the Perpendicular, or late Gothic style, is thought by some to have come about through the Black Death. As a result, much stone work fell to inexperienced masons who found the curving lines of the High Gothic style too demanding. But others point out that the essential features of the new style were evident 15 years before the onset of the Plague.

Left:
Ely Cathedral, Cambridgeshire
Ely derives its name from 'Eel Island', a reference to the diet of the Saxons who once lived there. Situated with the rest of the city on a hill rising from the surrounding fens, the cathedral is visible for miles around. Work on it was begun in 1083 on the site of a 7th century Benedictine abbey. King's School, the buildings below the cathedral here, was founded by Henry VIII but claims descent from the school attended by Edward the Confessor.

Above:
Stretham Engine House, Cambridgeshire
The first steam-engines to work pumps for the Fens drainage system were installed after 1817 but this one at Stretham on the River Great Ouse, dates from about 1830. It is maintained by a trust and is open to the public.

Above:

The Abbey, Bury St Edmunds, Suffolk

The abbey is the final resting place of St Edmund, King of East Anglia who was murdered by the Danes at Hoxne in Norfolk in AD870. His remains were transported to a number of places before arriving finally at the monastery of Beodricsworth in what was to become St Edmundsbury and later Bury St Edmunds. It was there, at the great altar in 1214, that the 25 barons vowed to extract from King John the concessions set out in the Magna Carta.

63

Right:

The Guildhall, Hadleigh, Suffolk
Hadleigh is yet another Suffolk town
which did well from the medieval wool
trade and the High Street has a range of
interesting buildings which date from that
period. But the Guildhall in Church
Square, built in 1430, is the most
distinguished.

Far right:

Framlingham Castle, Suffolk
The castle was built towards the end of the
12th century by Roger Bigod, the second
Earl of Norfolk. Under Henry VIII, it
became a royal castle; under Elizabeth 1, it
was a prison for Catholic priests. The
Castle's design hinged on the curtain wall,
rather than the keep, as the principal line
of defence, an idea picked up by the
Crusaders in the Levant and already by
then adopted in the royal castles at Dover
and Windsor. Bigod, not being short of
money, used vast quantities of limestone
from Northamptonshire which came up
the River Ore in barges.

Right:
Orford Castle, Suffolk
Orford Castle, begun in 1165, was
an attempt by Henry II to control
the recalcitrant Bigod, Earl of
Norfolk who controlled much of
Suffolk from Framlingham Castle.
Its construction transformed a
small fishing village into an
important port. Only the keep now
remains. Orford Ness, a sandspit
formed by the River Alde which
runs parallel to the coast before
emerging at Shingle Street to the
south, was controlled by the
military from the 1930s until
recently and some disused military
structures still remain there. It is
now administered by the National
Trust and is open to the public by
arrangement. Ferries run from
Orford Quay.

LANDSCAPES

Above:

Newmarket Heath, Suffolk/Cambridgeshire
Racehorses exercise on Newmarket Heath against a watery sunrise in early
winter. The town of Newmarket, itself in a narrow neck of Suffolk which juts
into Cambridgeshire — although the Heath pictured here is actually in
Cambridgeshire — is synonymous with horse-racing. James I first established
a Royal sporting connection, coming for the hare-coursing and hawking and
to escape London. His son, Charles I, continued the patronage but it was
Charles II who began the focus on matters equestrian.

67

Far left:
Near Ringstead, Northwest Norfolk
The landscape of this part of the
county is influenced by the underlying
chalk which is nearer to the surface
than elsewhere in Norfolk; the soil is
mostly light and sandy. While not a
true 'downland' landscape — the
finishing touches brought by arable
farming have seen to that — the area is
nevertheless characterised by wide
and expansive fields and a distinctive
sense of space.

Left:
Hunstanton, Northwest Norfolk
The chalk appears spectacularly in the
cliffs in the northern part of
Hunstanton where it overlays layers of
red chalk and carstone.

Above:
Near Beeston, central West Norfolk
There is more rolling and open country in the central western part of the
county, but here, near Beeston, the soil is heavier and the land would have
once been heavily wooded. Beeston church, one of the few in Norfolk with a
spire, is nearly a mile from the village but this is thought to be due to a steady
migration of the village to the edge of the large common which once served
the population, rather than any effect of the Black Death.

Right:
The Glaven Valley, North Norfolk
The River Glaven runs for barely a dozen miles, rising near Baconsthorpe and
reaching the sea near Blakeney where it is a major influence on the formation
and maintenance of Blakeney Point. On the way, it contributes greatly to the
landscaping of the grounds of Bayfield Hall.

Above:
The River Ant at Ludham Bridge, Norfolk Broads
The area known as the Norfolk Broads encompasses the Yare, Ant, Bure and Thurne river systems in East Norfolk and the Waveney which forms part of the boundary with Suffolk. The 'broads' themselves, lakes most of which connect with an adjacent river, are flooded peat diggings dating from the 12th to the 14th centuries. Collectively, the rivers and broads make an area for recreational boating which attracts more than two million visitors a year.

Right:
Early morning at Somerton Staithe, Norfolk Broads
If, in high season and in the busiest parts, the Broads can be a little hectic, there are always quiet backwaters for those who would seek peace and quiet.

Above:

A Breckland landscape, east of Mildenhall, Suffolk
Breckland straddles Northwest Suffolk and Southwest Norfolk, an area of about 400sq miles which in its natural state is relatively infertile, sandy heathland. Its distinctive nature has attracted some species of flora and fauna which are unknown elsewhere in the country. The name came from large flint-strewn open fields known locally as Brecks. Lines of Scots pine are a recurring feature, mostly planted in the 18th and 19th centuries as windbreaks and soil retainers.

THE FENS

The Fens comprise a vast area of former marshland left by the retreating glaciers of the Ice Ages which runs south and west from the coast of the Wash embracing Southwest Norfolk and large parts of Cambridgeshire and Lincolnshire. Attempts at drainage began with the Romans but in the 17th century, the fourth Earl of Bedford, whose family had been given the abbey estates of Thorney and Whittlesey in the western Fens after the Dissolution, was empowered by Royal Charter to turn this wasteland into good summer pasture. He hired the Dutch engineer, Cornelius Vermuyden, and eventually the canal known as the Old Bedford River was built and then supplemented in 1651 by the New Bedford River. Old and New run close together and almost parallel from Earith (between Huntingdon and Ely) to Denver Sluice, Southwest of Downham Market, where they join the River Great Ouse and then flow into the Wash at King's Lynn.

Other drains were built in succeeding centuries and the result is an extremely fertile landscape which is at once expansive, two-dimensional, locally remote and yet intensively cultivated almost to the last square inch. In winter it can be bleak and frozen and, at a time of global warming and rising sea levels, the threat of new inundation is ever present.

Above:
Power lines near Nordelph emphasise the flatness of the Fens.

75

Above:
Winter on the Old Bedford River at Welches Dam, Cambridgeshire

Right:
The New Bedford River, or Hundred Foot Drain, near Denver Sluice, Southwest Norfolk

Above:
A frosty morning near Coldham, north of March, Cambridgeshire.

Right:
The River Great Ouse, northwest of Over, Cambridgeshire.

Above:
Dusk, west of Outwell, Cambridgeshire